ANCIENT MYTHOLOGY

CHINESE MYTHS AND LEGENDS

by Janie Havemeyer
illustrated by Cesar Samaniego

GRASSHOPPER

Tools for Parents & Teachers

Grasshopper Books enhance imagination and introduce the earliest readers to fun storylines and illustrations. The easy-to-read text supports early reading experiences with repetitive sentence patterns and sight words.

Before Reading

- Discuss the cover illustration. What do readers see?
- Look at the glossary together. Discuss the words.

During Reading

- "Walk" through the book with the reader. Discuss new or unfamiliar words. Sound them out together.
- Look at the illustrations. When and where does the story take place? What is happening in the story?

After Reading

- Prompt the child to think more. Ask: What is your favorite Chinese myth? Why?

Grasshopper Books are published by Jump!
3500 American Blvd W, Suite 150
Bloomington, MN 55431
www.jumplibrary.com

Copyright © 2026 Jump! International copyright reserved in all countries. No part of this book may be reproduced in any form without written permission from the publisher.

Jump! is a division of FlutterBee Education Group.

Library of Congress Cataloging-in-Publication Data

Names: Havemeyer, Janie, author.
Samaniego, César, 1975- illustrator.
Title: Chinese myths and legends / by Janie Havemeyer; illustrated by Cesar Samaniego.
Description: Minneapolis, MN: Jump!, Inc., [2026]
Series: Ancient mythology | Includes index.
Audience: Ages 7-10
Identifiers: LCCN 2024047675 (print)
LCCN 2024047676 (ebook)
ISBN 9798892137508 (hardcover)
ISBN 9798892137515 (paperback)
ISBN 9798892137522 (ebook)
Subjects: LCSH: Mythology, Chinese–Juvenile literature.
Legends–Juvenile literature.
Folklore–Juvenile literature.
Classification: LCC BL1825 .H38 2026 (print)
LCC BL1825 (ebook)
DDC 398.20951–dc23/eng/20241121
LC record available at https://lccn.loc.gov/2024047675
LC ebook record available at https://lccn.loc.gov/2024047676

Editor: Alyssa Sorenson
Direction and Layout: Anna Peterson
Illustrator: Cesar Samaniego
Content Consultant: Nicholas Williams, PhD, Associate Professor of Chinese Literature, Arizona State University

Printed in the United States of America at Corporate Graphics in North Mankato, Minnesota.

Table of Contents

Gods, Heroes, and Dragons	4
Chinese Gods and Goddesses	22
To Learn More	23
Glossary	24
Index	24

Gods, Heroes, and Dragons

The Jade **Emperor** ruled heaven. He met with other Chinese gods and goddesses. They had important jobs. Gods who did a good job got happiness and luck! Gods who did not were punished.

Ancient Chinese people thought gods, like Mazu, could help them. Mazu had power over the sea. She protected fishermen. Other gods could hurt people. Stories about gods and heroes are known as **mythology**.

Lei Gong was the god of thunder. He punished people who did bad things. One day, two robbers stole from a man who was blind. Lei Gong beat a drum loudly as a warning. It sounded like thunder. The robbers did not stop, so Lei Gong hit them with a hammer. Since then, thunder reminds people to be good.

The Yellow Emperor was a god who ruled half the world. He battled Yan Di, the god of fire, for the other half. The Yellow Emperor led animals into battle. He won!

The Yellow Emperor ruled for many years. He is an **ancestor** of Chinese people. When he was done ruling Earth, he rode a dragon to heaven!

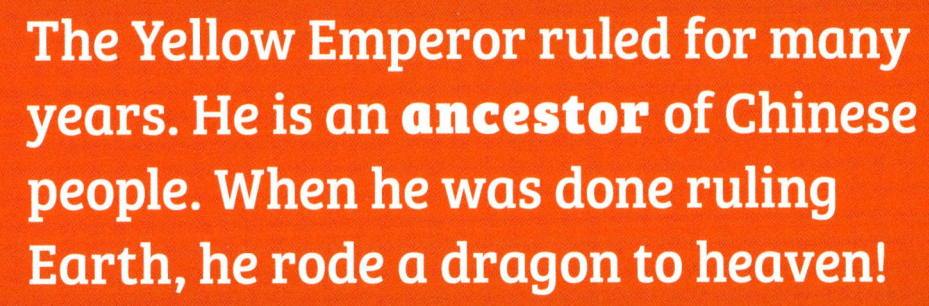

The dragon king ruled the water. His children could change from dragons to fish. One day, his son got caught in a fishing net. The prince cried for help. But once the prince was out of the water, the dragon king could not do anything.

Guanyin was the goddess of **compassion**. She heard the dragon prince's cries. The fisherman knew he had caught a magic fish. He tried to sell it. But Guanyin returned the prince to the sea.

The Yellow River kept flooding. It destroyed **crops**. People were starving. Yu was a king. He wanted to help.

Yu had a special power. He could change into a huge bear. He split a mountain in half with his paws. He made a new path for the river. It stopped flooding the land!

Mazu was once a girl named Lin Mo. Her **spirit** could travel to other places. One day, her family got trapped in a storm. Lin Mo's spirit tried to show them the way home. But her brother fell into the sea.

After her death, Lin Mo became the goddess Mazu. She could better help people at sea.

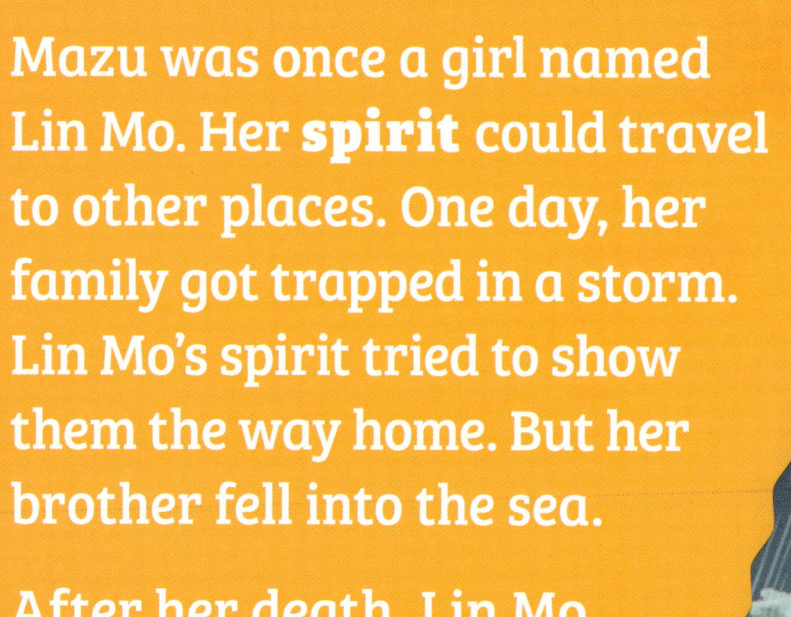

Once, there were 10 suns in the sky. Their heat burned crops. Rivers dried up. Rocks melted.

Yi was a brave hero. He shot down nine of the suns. Only one was left in the sky. The world was balanced again!

Yi got a magic pill. It could make him live forever. His wife, Chang'e, accidentally swallowed it. She floated into the sky. She landed on the Moon. It became her home. She became the Moon goddess.

Chang'e and Yi saw each other during the full Moon. Now, people **reunite** with loved ones during the Moon Festival every year!

Chinese Gods and Goddesses

Who are Chinese mythology's most important gods and goddesses? Take a look!

Chang'e
Moon goddess

dragon king
God of water, weather, and dragons

Guandi
God of war

Guanyin
Goddess of compassion

Jade Emperor
Ruler of heaven

Lei Gong
God of thunder

Mazu
Goddess of the sea and protector of sailors, fishermen, and travelers

Yan Di
God of fire

Yellow Emperor
First god-emperor of China and ancestor of Chinese people

To Learn More

Finding more information is as easy as 1, 2, 3.
1. Go to www.factsurfer.com
2. Enter "**Chinesemythsandlegends**" into the search box.
3. Choose your book to see a list of websites.

Glossary

ancestor: A member of one's family who lived long ago.

ancient: Very old or from the very distant past.

compassion: A feeling of sympathy for and a desire to help someone who is suffering.

crops: Plants grown for food.

emperor: A male ruler of an empire.

mythology: A group of stories from a particular culture or religion.

reunite: To come together again.

spirit: The part of a person that is believed to control thoughts and feelings.

Index

bear 15

Chang'e 20

dragon king 10

Guanyin 12

heaven 4, 9

Jade Emperor 4

Lei Gong 6

Mazu 5, 16

Moon Festival 20

sea 5, 12, 16

spirit 16

Yan Di 8

Yellow Emperor 8, 9

Yellow River 14, 15

Yi 18, 20

Yu 14, 15